# THE BEATLES

Arranged by Chad Johnson

ISBN 978-1-5400-5743-3

Visit Hal Leonard Online at
**www.halleonard.com**

Contact us:
**Hal Leonard**
7777 West Bluemound Road
Milwaukee, WI 53213
Email: info@halleonard.com

In Europe, contact:
**Hal Leonard Europe Limited**
42 Wigmore Street
Marylebone, London, W1U 2RN
Email: info@halleonardeurope.com

In Australia, contact:
**Hal Leonard Australia Pty. Ltd.**
4 Lentara Court
Cheltenham, Victoria, 3192 Australia
Email: info@halleonard.com.au

# ALL MY LOVING

Words and Music by John Lennon and Paul McCartney

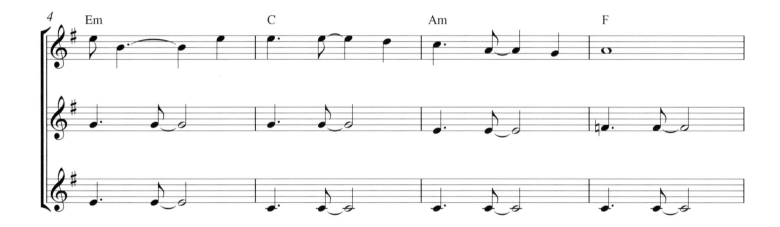

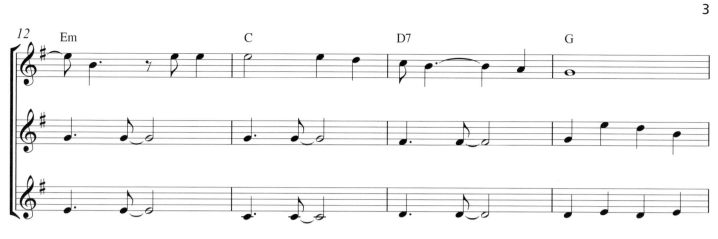

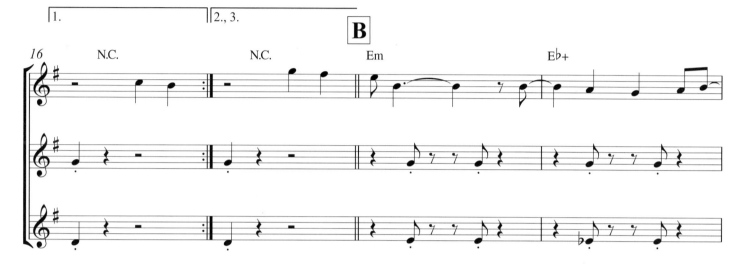

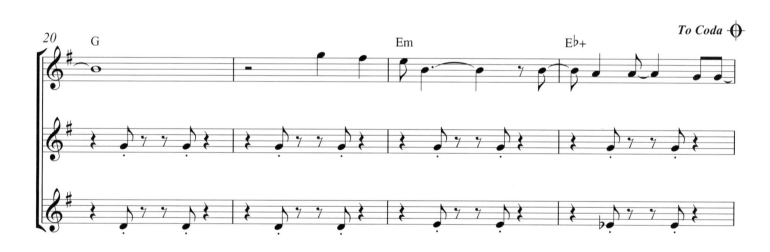

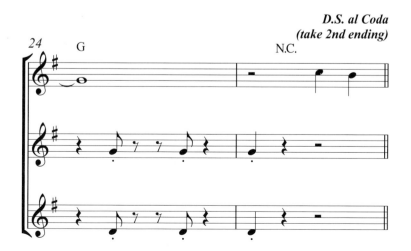

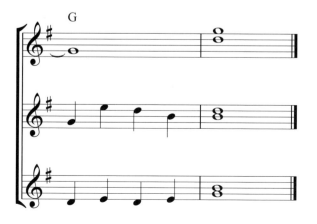

# BLACKBIRD

*Words and Music by John Lennon and Paul McCartney*

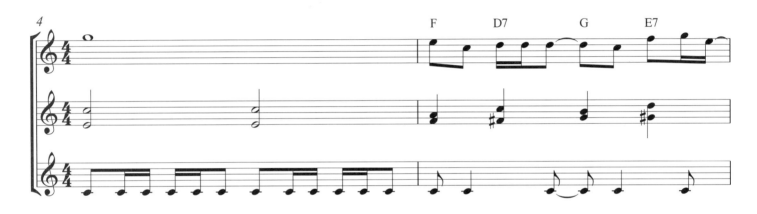

**B**

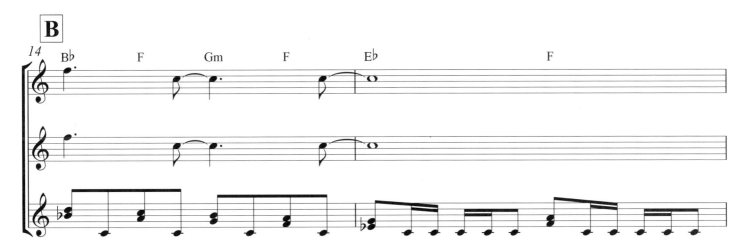

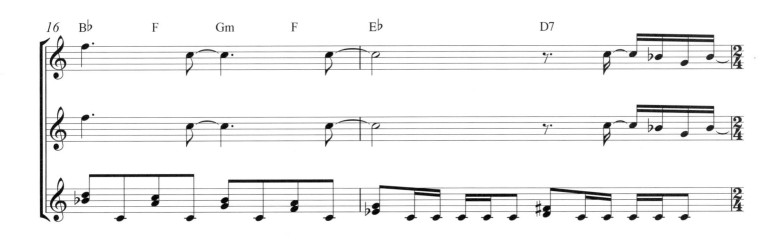

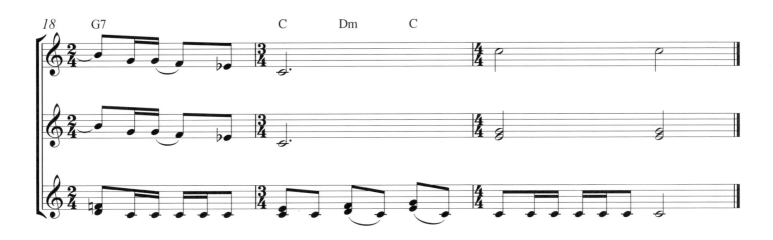

# CAN'T BUY ME LOVE

Words and Music by John Lennon and Paul McCartney

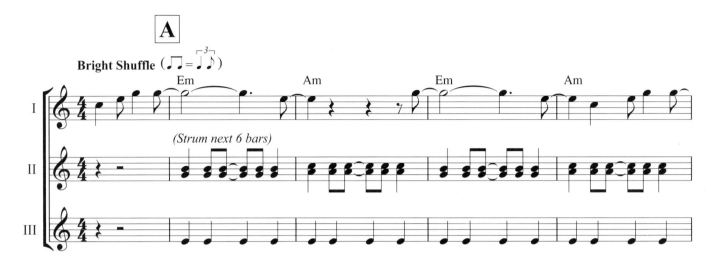

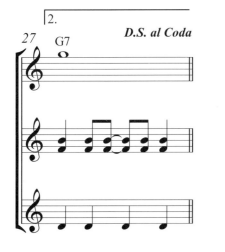

# EIGHT DAYS A WEEK

Words and Music by John Lennon and Paul McCartney

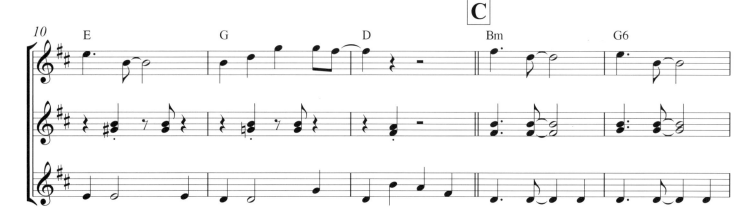

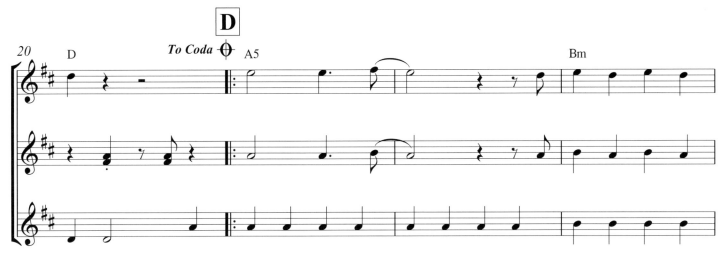

# HERE, THERE AND EVERYWHERE

Words and Music by John Lennon and Paul McCartney

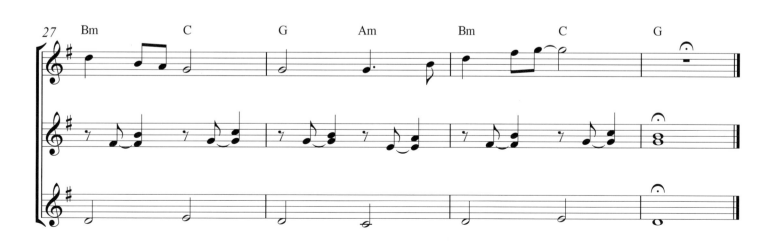

# I WANT TO HOLD YOUR HAND

Words and Music by John Lennon and Paul McCartney

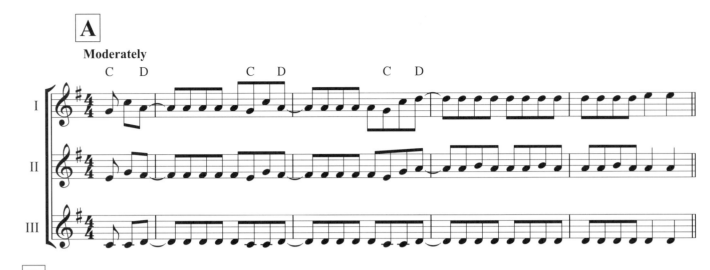

**D**

*2nd time, D.S. al Coda*

**Coda**

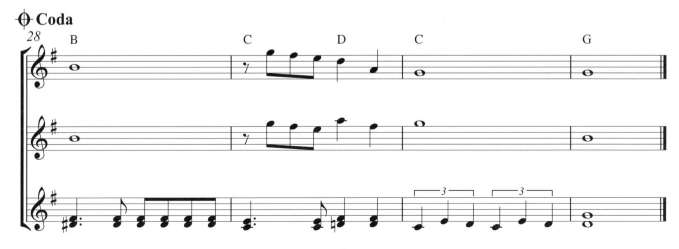

# LET IT BE

Words and Music by John Lennon and Paul McCartney

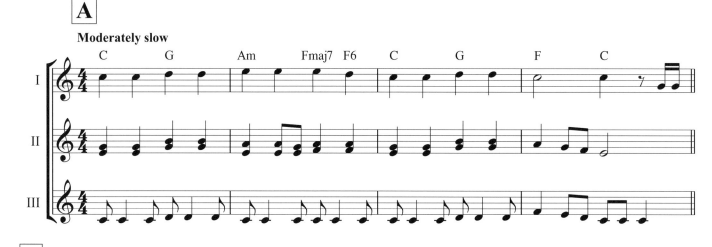

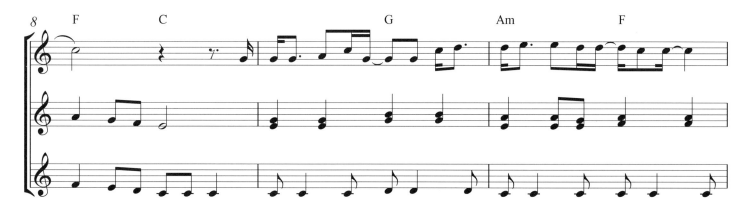

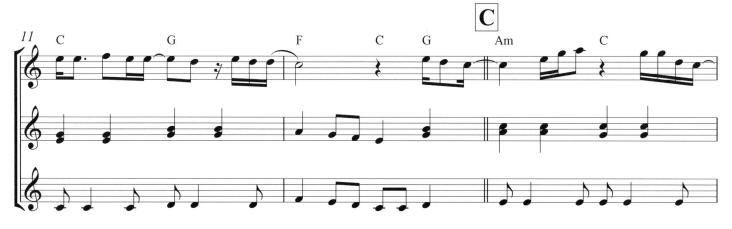

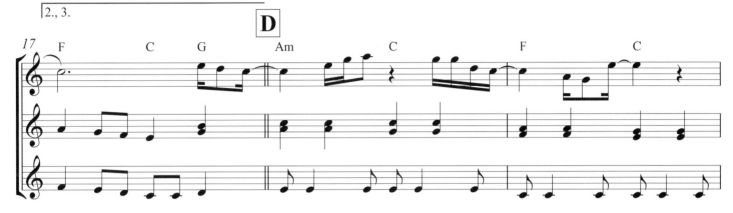

# LOVE ME DO

Words and Music by John Lennon and Paul McCartney

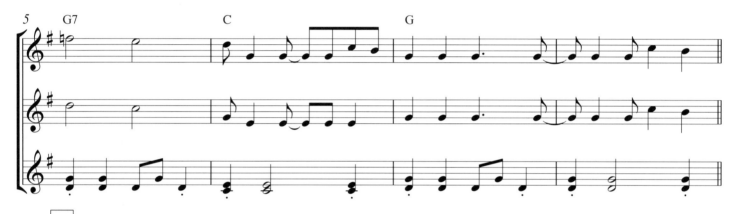

# NORWEGIAN WOOD
## (This Bird Has Flown)

Words and Music by John Lennon and Paul McCartney

# PENNY LANE

Words and Music by John Lennon and Paul McCartney

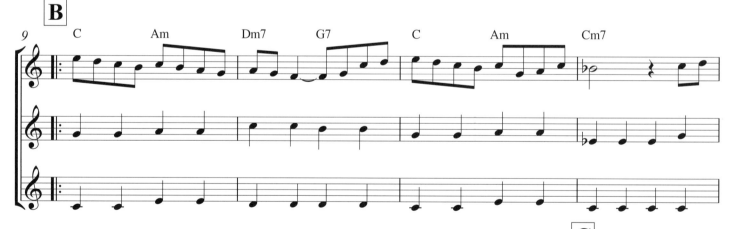

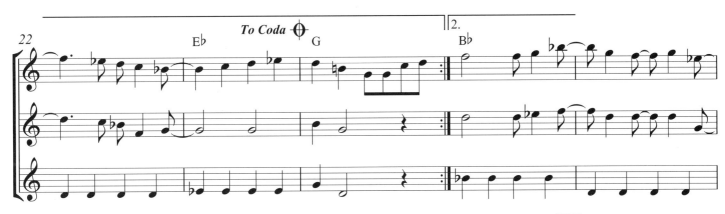

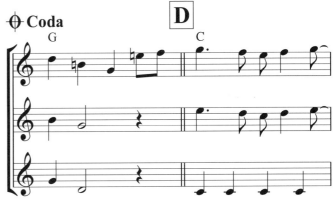

# SOMETHING

Words and Music by George Harrison

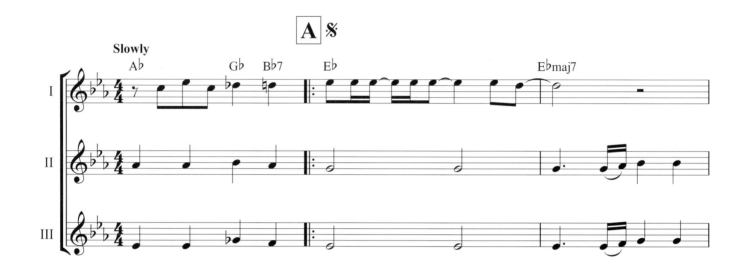

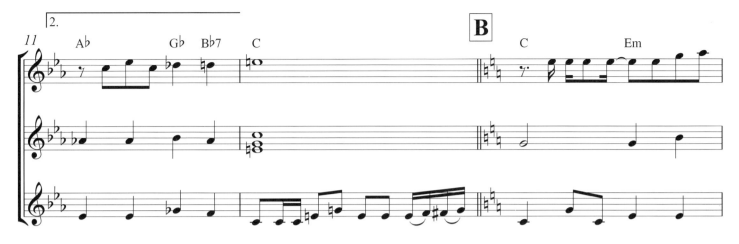

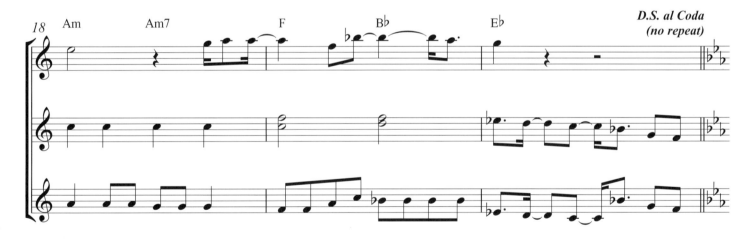

# TICKET TO RIDE

Words and Music by John Lennon and Paul McCartney

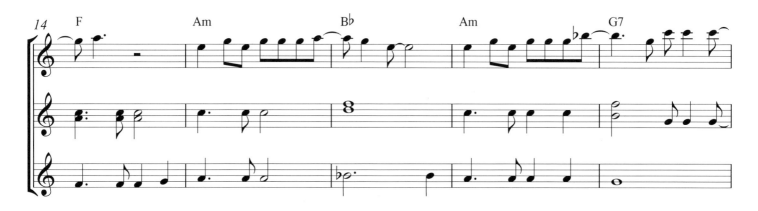

# WHEN I'M SIXTY-FOUR

Words and Music by John Lennon and Paul McCartney

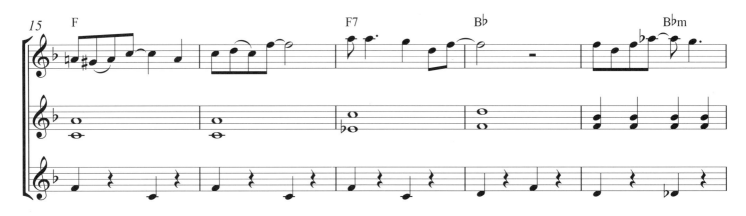

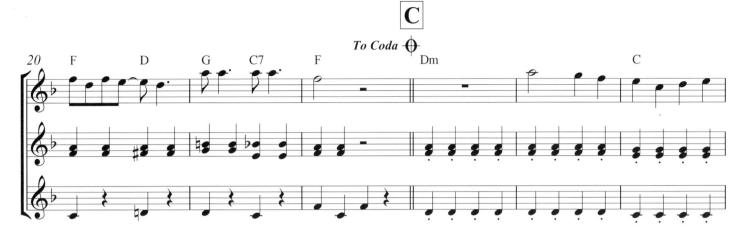

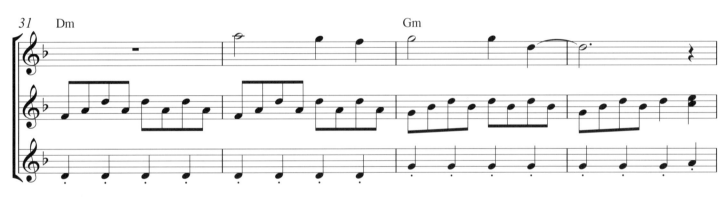

# YELLOW SUBMARINE

Words and Music by John Lennon and Paul McCartney

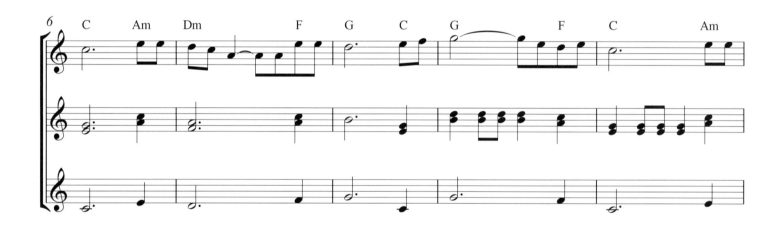

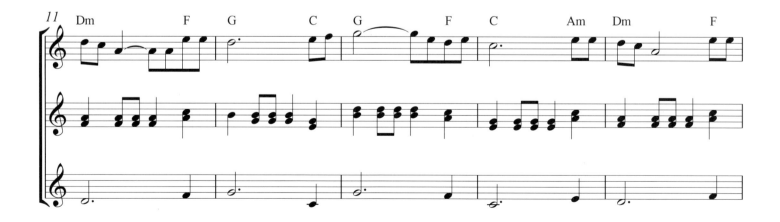

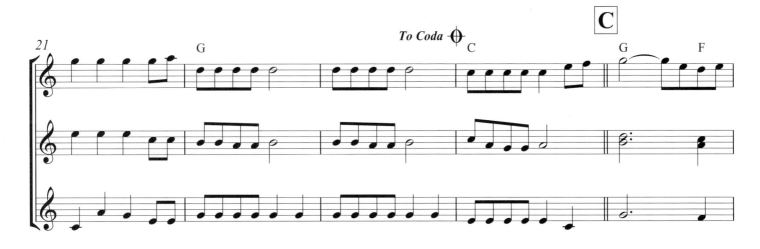

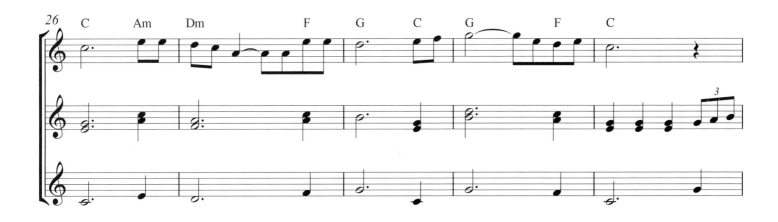

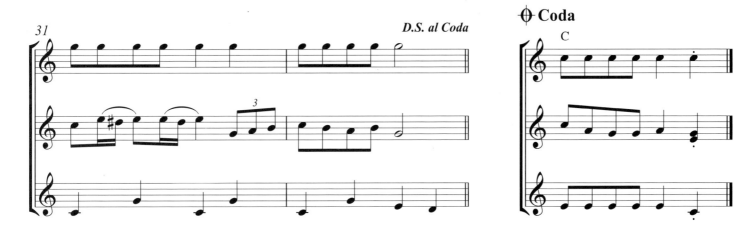

# YESTERDAY

Words and Music by John Lennon and Paul McCartney

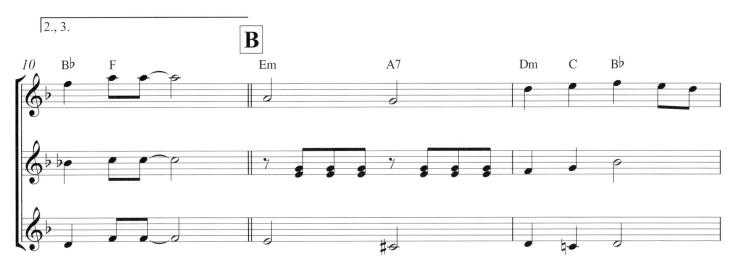

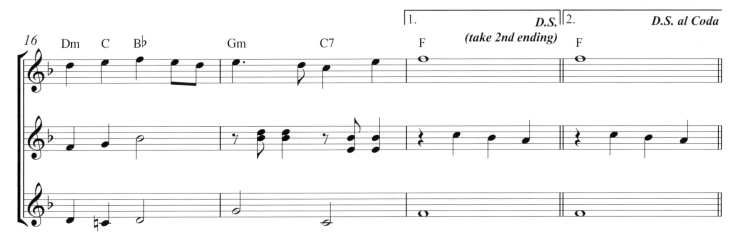

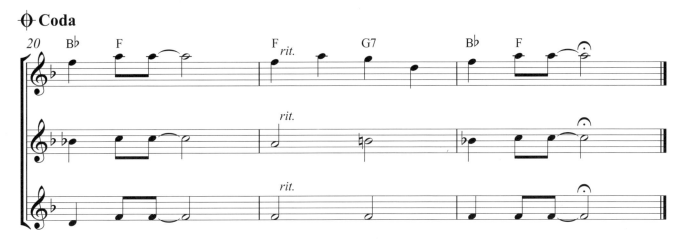

## NOTES FROM THE ARRANGER

Arranging for three ukuleles can be challenging because of the instrument's limited range. In standard tuning (G-C-E-A), there is only one octave plus a major sixth between the open C string and fret 12 on the A string. Certain melodies easily span this distance and more, so compromises sometimes had to be made.

Not all ukuleles have the same number of frets. If your uke has fewer than 15 frets, you may need to play certain phrases an octave lower (especially in Part I). Some phrases have already been transposed up or down an octave—this was only done out of necessity and kept to a minimum. A few songs require every inch of available fretboard, but fret 15 on the first string (high C) is the limit, and this is extremely rare.

The three voices will sometimes cross as a result of range limitations. If Part III is considered to be the "bass" line, keep in mind that the lowest available "bass" notes are sometimes on the first string! However, if you own a baritone ukulele, almost all of the notes in Part III could be played an octave lower (except the open C string and C# on fret 1), thus providing a more effective bass line.

Despite the above caveats, I believe that the spirit of these songs has been preserved, and I hope you enjoy playing these arrangements as much as I enjoyed creating them. By the way, a fourth ensemble part can be added by strumming along with the chord symbols!

– Chad Johnson

### SOPRANO, CONCERT & TENOR FRETBOARD

### BARITONE FRETBOARD

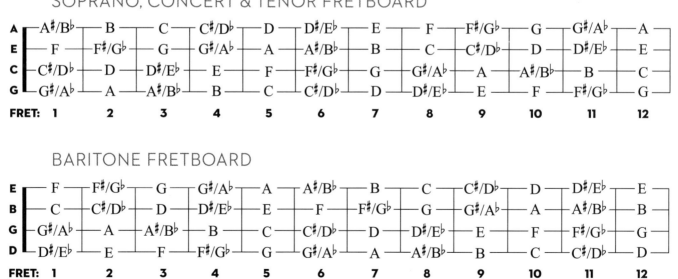